DREAMING BIG TOGETHER PUBLISHING PRESENTS

THE
DIAGNOSIS

GETTING TO THE ROOT OF THE PROBLEM

WRITTEN BY

SABRINA BEN SALMI

THE
DIAGNOSIS

GETTING TO THE ROOT OF THE PROBLEM

Published by Dreaming Big Together Publishing

DREAMING BIG TOGETHER PUBLISHING PRESENTS

THE
DIAGNOSIS

GETTING TO THE ROOT OF THE PROBLEM

WRITTEN BY

SABRINA BEN SALMI

What is a diagnosis?

"diagnosis (of something) the act of discovering or identifying the exact cause of an illness or a problem.

- Oxfordlearnersdictionary.com

ACKNOWLEDGEMENTS

ACKNOWLEDGEMENTS

Writing a book is never a solitary endeavour; it is a culmination of inspiration, support, and collaboration. "The Diagnosis - Getting to the Root Cause" has been a labour of love, and I am grateful to the many individuals who have contributed to its creation.

First and foremost, I extend my deepest gratitude to my family for their unwavering encouragement and understanding throughout this journey. Your belief in me and my ideas has been a constant source of motivation.

I am indebted to my family, friends and colleagues who provided invaluable insights and discussions that enriched the content of this book. Your diverse perspectives challenged me to think critically and deeply about the concepts presented. To the experts and professionals who generously shared their knowledge and experiences, thank you for being the guiding light in unravelling the complexities of personal and professional problems. Your wisdom has been instrumental in shaping the ideas within these pages. My heartfelt appreciation goes to my editor and my entire publishing team who dedicated their time and expertise to refine and polish this manuscript. Your dedication to excellence has transformed my words into a coherent and impactful narrative. I would like to express gratitude to the readers who will engage with this book. Your curiosity and willingness to explore new ideas inspire me to continue my quest for understanding and insight.

Lastly, I acknowledge the countless individuals who have faced personal and professional challenges head-on, teaching us all the importance of seeking the root cause. May this book serve as a tool to empower you on your journey of self-discovery and growth.

With profound appreciation,

Sabrina Ben Salmi

DEDICATION

DEDICATION

I dedicate this book to all those who have dared to ask "why?" and to those who have ventured beyond the surface to uncover the hidden truths.

This book is dedicated to the seekers of understanding, wisdom, thought-provoking truth, the champions of growth, and the advocates of change. Your relentless pursuit of the root cause has illuminated the path to solutions, offering clarity in the face of complexity.

May the insights within these pages empower you to navigate the intricate terrain of personal and professional challenges, and may your commitment to unravelling the mysteries of the human experience continue to inspire us all.

With admiration and respect,

- Sabrina Ben Salmi

INTRODUCTION

1. INTRODUCTION

In today's fast-paced and complex world, it is not uncommon for individuals and businesses to face persistent problems that seem to defy all attempts at resolution. Despite countless diagnoses and attempts at solving these problems, the root causes often remain unidentified, leading to ineffective solutions and ongoing challenges. This book aims to change that by providing a step-by-step process for defining and diagnosing problems, with a focus on uncovering the underlying issues that contribute to their persistence. By understanding the importance of identifying the root problems, readers will be equipped with the tools and strategies necessary to address the challenges they face and achieve optimal solutions.

Understanding the diagnosis process is key to resolving persistent problems. Through this book, readers will dive into the art of defining specific life or business problems they are encountering, uncovering the challenges they present. By being as detailed as possible in describing these challenges, readers will gain clarity on the complexities and intricacies that lie beneath the surface. The step-by-step process presented in this book aims to guide readers towards improvement strategies that are both effective and practical, ultimately leading to growth and success in both personal and professional endeavors.

1.1 UNDERSTANDING THE DIAGNOSIS PROCESS

The diagnosis process is a crucial step in identifying and addressing the root causes of persistent problems. It involves a systematic approach to analyzing and understanding the challenges that individuals or businesses face in their daily lives. By thoroughly examining the symptoms and underlying causes of a problem, individuals can develop effective strategies for finding optimal solutions.

One key aspect of understanding the diagnosis process is recognizing the importance of thoroughness and attention to detail. Often, surface-level analysis of a problem can lead to superficial solutions that merely address the symptoms rather than the underlying causes. For example, imagine a business experiencing a decline in sales. A quick diagnosis might conclude that the problem is due to poor customer service. However, a more in-depth analysis may uncover that the root cause is actually an ineffective marketing strategy. By delving deeper into the underlying causes, organizations can develop targeted solutions that address the true source of the problem.

Effective diagnosis also involves gathering and analyzing relevant data. This data might include customer feedback, sales reports, or industry trends. By utilizing data-driven insights, individuals can form a comprehensive view of the problem at hand and make informed decisions based on evidence. For example, analyzing customer feedback might reveal common pain points that can be addressed through product improvements or enhanced customer service.

To aid in the diagnosis process, individuals can also leverage external resources and references. Industry research, case studies, and expert opinions can provide valuable insights and perspectives. For example, a business facing challenges with employee retention might consult studies on workplace satisfaction and employee engagement to better understand

The underlying factors contributing to turnover. By incorporating external references and expert knowledge, individuals can enhance their understanding of the problem and identify effective strategies for improvement.

Overall, understanding the diagnosis process is crucial for identifying and addressing the root causes of persistent problems. By taking a systematic approach, being thorough in analysis, gathering relevant data, and leveraging external resources, individuals can gain a deep understanding of the challenges they face and develop effective strategies for improvement.

External references:
- Johnson, S. (2018). The Thinking Person's Guide to Sobriety. Random House. Here is the link to the book: https://www.penguinrandomhouse.com/books/316108/the-thinking-persons-guide-to-sobriety-by-aaa-simon-johnson/

- Harvard Business Review. (2017). "The Importance of Data-Driven Decision Making." Here is the link to the book: https://hbr.org/2017/06/the-importance-of-data-driven-decision-making

1.2 IMPORTANCE OF IDENTIFYING ROOT PROBLEMS

Identifying the root problem is a critical step in the diagnosis process because it allows us to address the underlying cause of a persistent issue rather than just treating the symptoms. By understanding the root problem, we can develop more effective and long-term solutions that truly resolve the issue at hand.

One of the main reasons why identifying root problems is important is the fact that it helps avoid the phenomenon of "diagnosis often problem persists." Often, when faced with a problem, we tend to focus on the immediate symptoms or surface-level issues without considering the deeper cause. This can result in temporary fixes that do not fully resolve the problem, leading to its persistence. For example, imagine a manufacturing company experiencing a decrease in productivity. The immediate reaction might be to blame the employees for not being efficient enough. However, upon closer inspection, it is discovered that the outdated machinery and lack of training are the root causes of the decreased productivity. By identifying these root problems, the company can invest in new equipment and provide appropriate training, leading to a significant improvement in productivity. Another reason why identifying root problems is important is that it allows us to eliminate unnecessary and ineffective solutions. Without understanding the root cause, we might implement solutions that do not address the core issue, resulting in wasted time, effort, and resources. To illustrate this, let's consider a scenario where an individual is trying to lose weight but is struggling despite following popular diets and exercise routines. By identifying the root problem, which could be emotional eating triggered by stress, the individual can seek therapy or develop coping mechanisms to address the underlying cause. This targeted approach is more likely to lead to successful weight loss compared to blindly following generic diet plans.

In conclusion, identifying root problems is crucial in the diagnosis process because it enables us to find lasting and effective solutions. By understanding the underlying causes of persistent issues, we can develop targeted strategies that address the core problem, leading to meaningful and sustainable improvements.

References:

- Rogers, R. (2016). The Importance of Identifying the Root Cause of a Problem. Mind Tools. Retrieved from: https://www.mindtools.com/pages/article/newTMC_80.htm

- Strickland, J. (2020). The Importance of Identifying the Root Cause of a Problem in Business. Houston Chronicle. Retrieved from:
https://www.mindtools.com/pages/article/newTMC_80.htm

1.3 OVERVIEW OF THE STEP-BY-STEP PROCESS

The step-by-step process outlined in this book is designed to help individuals and organizations identify and address the root causes of persistent problems. By following a structured approach, readers will be guided towards optimal solutions and improvement strategies that can lead to significant positive changes in their personal and business lives.

The process begins with clearly defining the specific life or business problem facing the individual or organization. This involves articulating the challenges and obstacles that are being encountered. By providing a detailed description of the problem, it becomes easier to understand the underlying issues that need to be addressed.

Once the problem is defined, the next step is to gather relevant data. This may involve conducting interviews, surveys, or analyzing existing information. By collecting and analyzing data, it becomes possible to gain a deeper understanding of the problem and identify potential causes.

Root cause analysis is a crucial step in the process. It involves identifying the root cause factors that contribute to the problem. This may require evaluating contributing factors and mapping cause-and-effect relationships. By uncovering the underlying causes of the problem, it becomes possible to develop effective solutions that address the root issues.

Guiding the next steps involves setting priorities for solutions and generating innovative ideas. It is important to assess the feasibility of the proposed solutions and develop action plans for implementation. This step also includes considering the execution of action plans, monitoring and evaluation, and making adjustments as needed. The book also covers improvement strategies that promote a continuous improvement mindset. Building a culture of innovation and leveraging technology for improvement are explored, along with scaling-up solutions for maximum impact.

Overall, this step-by-step process provides a roadmap for readers to diagnose problems effectively and guide them towards finding optimal solutions and improvement strategies. By following this process, individuals and organizations can unlock potential for growth and success.

For further reading on problem-solving and decision-making processes, the following references may be helpful:

- Mauboussin, M. J. (2012). Think Twice: Harnessing the Power of Counterintuition. Harvard Business Press: https://www.amazon.com/Think-Twice-Harnessing-Counterintuition-Harvard/dp/1422176755
- Duhigg, C. (2012). The Power of Habit: Why We Do What We Do in Life and Business. Random House: https://www.amazon.com/Power-Habit-What-Life-Business/dp/081298160X
- Christensen, C. M. (1997). The Innovator's Dilemma: When New Technologies Cause Great Firms to Fail. Harvard Business Review Press:

https://www.amazon.com/Innovators-Dilemma-Technologies-Management-Innovation/dp/1633691780

These resources offer valuable insights and frameworks for understanding and improving problem-solving processes in personal and business contexts.

2 IDENTIFYING THE PROBLEM

In order to find effective solutions, it is crucial to first identify and define the specific life or business problem at hand. This chapter provides a comprehensive guide on how to articulate and describe these challenges in detail. By clearly understanding the problem, individuals and organizations can then proceed towards finding optimal solutions and strategies for improvement.

By defining the specific life problem, readers will gain a deeper understanding of the challenges they are facing on a personal level. Whether it is a problem related to relationships, health, or personal growth, this chapter will help individuals articulate their challenges and analyze the root causes. Additionally, the chapter also explores how to define specific business problems, enabling readers to identify the issues that are hindering their organization's success.

Furthermore, this chapter emphasizes the importance of being as detailed as possible when describing the challenges one is facing. By examining the problem from various angles and considering all relevant factors, individuals and organizations can better understand the underlying issues. This comprehensive understanding of the problem is essential for guiding the next steps towards optimal solutions and improvement strategies.

2.1 DEFINING THE SPECIFIC LIFE PROBLEM

Defining the specific life problem is a crucial step in the diagnosis process as it lays the foundation for identifying the root cause and devising effective solutions. In this section, we will explore the importance of clearly articulating the life problems facing individuals and provide examples to illustrate this concept.

When defining a specific life problem, it is important to be as detailed as possible in describing the challenges faced. This requires careful observation and reflection on the symptoms, patterns, and underlying issues that contribute to the problem.

Let's consider an example to understand the process of defining a specific life problem. Suppose an individual is experiencing chronic fatigue and a lack of motivation in their daily life. They may start by describing their symptoms in detail, such as feeling tired even after getting enough sleep, lacking energy to perform daily tasks, and experiencing a constant sense of lethargy. Next, the individual needs to dig deeper and identify the potential causes contributing to their fatigue and lack of motivation. This could include factors such as a demanding work schedule, unhealthy lifestyle habits, unresolved emotional issues, or an underlying medical condition. By identifying these contributing factors, the individual can gain a better understanding of the root cause of their problem.

Once the specific life problem has been clearly defined, the individual can then proceed to analyze the problem and develop appropriate solutions. This may involve seeking professional help, making lifestyle changes, addressing emotional issues through therapy, or seeking medical treatment. By addressing the root cause of the problem, individuals can find long-lasting solutions and improve their overall well-being.

It is worth noting that defining the specific life problem requires self-awareness and introspection. It may be helpful to journal, seek feedback from trusted friends or family members, or consult with experts in relevant fields to gain additional insights into the problem.

To further enhance your understanding of defining specific life problems, you may refer to the following external resources:

- "Identifying the Key Problems You Face," an article by Mind Tools, provides practical tips on identifying and defining specific problems in various aspects of life. https://www.mindtools.com/pages/article/key-problems.htm
- "How to Define a Problem: A New Framework for Innovation," a TED Talk by Daria Crocco, discusses the importance of clearly defining problems to drive innovation and offers a framework for problem-solving. Here is the link to the TED Talk: https://www.ted.com/talks/daria_crocco_how_to_define_a_problem_a_new_framework_for_innovation

Defining the specific life problem is a crucial step that sets the stage for the subsequent stages of the diagnosis process. By articulating the challenges faced, individuals can gain a deeper understanding of the root causes and ultimately find effective solutions for personal growth and improvement.

2.2 DEFINING THE SPECIFIC BUSINESS PROBLEM

Defining the specific business problem is a crucial step in the diagnosis process. It involves identifying and articulating the specific challenges or obstacles faced by a business that hinder its growth, profitability, or overall success. By clearly defining the problem, businesses can gain a deeper understanding of what needs to be addressed and develop effective strategies to overcome it.

To define the specific business problem, it is important to consider the following factors:

1. **Identifying the areas of concern:** Businesses need to identify the key areas or aspects of their operations that are causing problems. This could include issues related to sales, marketing, production, customer service, or financial management. By pinpointing the specific area of concern, businesses can narrow down their focus and develop targeted solutions. For example, a manufacturing company may identify that its production process is inefficient, leading to delays and increased costs. This becomes the specific business problem that needs to be addressed.

2. **Understanding the impact on business goals:** Defining the specific business problem requires businesses to understand how it affects their overall goals and objectives. This includes assessing the impact on revenue, customer satisfaction, employee morale, or market competitiveness. By understanding the consequences of the problem, businesses can prioritize its resolution and allocate resources accordingly. For instance, a retail store may realize that its outdated inventory management system is causing frequent stockouts, resulting in lost sales and dissatisfied customers. This negative impact on revenue and customer satisfaction makes it a specific business problem that needs immediate attention.

3. **Considering the external environment:** Businesses must

also consider the external factors that may contribute to the specific problem they are facing. This includes analyzing industry trends, customer preferences, competitive pressures, regulatory requirements, or technological advancements. By understanding these external influences, businesses can better address the root causes of their problems and develop strategies that align with the changing business landscape.

For example, a software company may find that its outdated software development practices are causing delays in releasing new products, while its competitors are introducing innovative features at a faster pace. This external pressure makes it essential for the company to define and solve the specific business problem to stay competitive.

By clearly defining the specific business problem, businesses can lay the foundation for effective problem-solving and improvement. It provides a starting point for gathering relevant data, analyzing potential causes, and determining the most appropriate solutions. With a well-defined problem, businesses can focus their efforts and resources on achieving optimal outcomes.

For more information on defining business problems, consider the following resources:

- Harvard Business Review: <u>The Art of Framing Problems</u>: https://hbr.org/2017/05/the-art-of-framing-problems
- Entrepreneur: <u>How to Define Business Goals and Objectives</u>: https://www.entrepreneur.com/article/290547

2.3 ARTICULATING THE CHALLENGES FACED

Articulating the challenges faced is a crucial step in the diagnosis process as it helps to clearly identify and understand the specific problems that need to be addressed. By describing the challenges in detail, individuals and businesses can gain a deeper insight into the root causes of their persistent problems and develop targeted solutions.

When articulating the challenges faced, it is important to be as specific and detailed as possible. For example, instead of simply stating that a business is experiencing a decline in sales, it would be more effective to provide specific information such as the products or services that have seen a decrease in demand, the target market segment that is being impacted, and any external factors that may be influencing the decline.

By providing specific details, individuals and businesses can better understand the complexity of the challenges they are facing and develop appropriate strategies to address them. For instance, if a business is experiencing a decline in sales due to increased competition, it may need to focus on developing a unique selling proposition or revising its marketing strategies to differentiate itself from competitors.

External references:
- This article from Harvard Business Review provides insights on the importance of articulating specific challenges in problem-solving: Articulating and Solving Highly Complicated Problems: https://hbr.org/2016/11/articulating-and-solving-highly-complicated-problems
- The book "The Art of Problem Solving: A Guide to Business Innovation" by Russell Ackoff and Herbert J. Addison offers strategies for articulating challenges and finding innovative solutions: The Art of Problem Solving: https://www.amazon.com/Art-Problem-Solving-Business-Innovation/dp/0471055589

- "Problem-Solving Skills for Success" by Kenneth Blanchard and Vincent T. Mastro provides practical techniques for identifying and articulating the challenges faced in personal and professional contexts: Problem Solving Skills for Success: https://www.amazon.com/Problem-Solving-Success-Kenneth-Blanchard/dp/013307830X

2.4 GATHERING RELEVANT DATA

Gathering relevant data is a crucial step in the diagnosis process. It involves collecting information and evidence that will help in understanding the problem at hand and identifying the root cause. By examining various types of data, individuals and organizations can gain valuable insights and make informed decisions about the best course of action.

There are several methods and sources that can be used to gather relevant data. Here are some examples:

1. **Surveys and Questionnaires:** Surveys and questionnaires can be designed to gather information from individuals who are directly involved in or affected by the problem. They can provide quantitative data, such as ratings or rankings, as well as qualitative data, such as comments or suggestions. Online survey platforms like SurveyMonkey or Google Forms can be used to create and distribute surveys easily.
2. **Interviews:** Conducting interviews allows for a more in-depth understanding of the problem and its underlying causes. Interviews can be structured or unstructured, depending on the specific needs and goals of the diagnosis process. They can be conducted face-to-face, over the phone, or through video conferencing tools like Zoom or Skype.
3. **Observations:** Direct observation of the problem and the surrounding environment can provide valuable insights. Observations can be done in-person or through video recordings. By carefully observing and documenting the behaviours, interactions, and patterns related to the problem, individuals and organizations can uncover hidden factors and patterns that may contribute to its persistence.
4. **Data Analysis:** Existing data within an organization's systems or publicly available data can be analyzed to

gain insights into the problem. This can include financial data, sales reports, customer feedback, and performance metrics. There are various data analysis tools and techniques that can be utilized, such as Microsoft Excel, Google Analytics, or data visualization software like Tableau.

5. External Research: In some cases, external research may be necessary to gather relevant data. This can involve reviewing academic journals, industry reports, or case studies that are related to the specific problem being diagnosed. External research provides additional context and insights that can enhance the understanding of the problem and guide the diagnosis process.

It is important to ensure that the data gathered is reliable, accurate, and relevant to the problem being diagnosed. Care should be taken to avoid biases or inaccuracies that could lead to flawed analysis and misguided solutions. Proper data collection and management techniques should be followed to maintain data integrity and privacy.

I.Eliot, G.P. (2017). "Researching organizational problems". Organizational Research Methods. 20 (3): 459–487. doi:10.1177/1094428116654562. Leveraging Technology for Data Collection and Analysis. (n.d.). Retrieved November 9, 2021, from https://www.analyticbridge.datasciencecentral.com/profiles/blogs/leveraging-technology-for-data-collection-and-analysis

2.5 ANALYZING EXISTING SOLUTIONS

Once the specific life or business problem has been defined and the challenges have been articulated, it is important to analyze existing solutions that have been implemented in the past. This step allows us to learn from previous attempts at addressing the problem and helps us identify any potential patterns or trends that may have contributed to the persistence of the problem.

Analyzing existing solutions involves gathering information about the strategies, methods, or techniques that have been utilized in the past to address the problem. This can be done through a variety of methods such as conducting interviews with stakeholders, reviewing historical data and reports, and examining case studies or success stories from similar contexts.

For example, if the problem is the high employee turnover rate in a company, the analysis of existing solutions may involve studying the strategies implemented by other companies to improve employee retention. This could include reviewing research articles on best practices, interviewing HR professionals from successful companies, and examining case studies of companies that have effectively reduced turnover.

By analyzing existing solutions, we can gain insights into what has worked and what has not worked in the past. This information helps us avoid repeating unsuccessful strategies and enables us to identify innovative approaches that have the potential to address the root cause of the problem.

External references:
- Harvard Business Review: Why Your Problem-Solving Efforts Fail: https://hbr.org/2017/09/why-your-problem-solving-efforts-fail

- Stanford Social Innovation Review: <u>Using Failure as a Learning Opportunity</u>:
  https://ssir.org/articles/entry/using_failure_as_a_learning_opportunity
- McKinsey & Company: <u>The Seven Step Problem Solving Process</u>:
  https://www.mckinsey.com/business-functions/operations/our-insights/the-seven-step-problem-solving-process

The analysis of existing solutions should also consider the context in which they were implemented. Factors such as organizational culture, resources available, and external influences can greatly impact the success or failure of a solution. Therefore, it is important to take a holistic view of the problem and consider the broader picture when analyzing existing solutions.

In conclusion, analyzing existing solutions provides valuable insights and lessons learned that can inform the development of effective strategies for addressing persistent problems. By taking into account past experiences and learning from both successes and failures, we can increase the likelihood of finding optimal solutions that address the root cause of the problem.

Next, we will move on to the next step in the process, which is conducting a root cause analysis.

3 ROOT CAUSE ANALYSIS

Root cause analysis is a crucial step in the diagnosis process, as it allows us to dive deeper into the underlying factors contributing to a persistent problem. By identifying these root causes, we can gain a better understanding of why the problem exists in the first place. This chapter will guide you through the process of identifying and evaluating these root cause factors, helping you uncover the true sources of the challenges you are facing.

In the pursuit of finding optimal solutions, it is important to distinguish between symptoms and root causes. While symptoms may be evident and easily identifiable, they are often just manifestations of deeper underlying issues. By conducting a systematic root cause analysis, you will be able to move beyond surface-level observations and delve into the core reasons for the problem.

This in-depth understanding forms the basis for effective problem-solving and ensures that your solutions address the actual source of the problem rather than just treating the symptoms.

Throughout this chapter, we will explore various techniques for identifying root causes, evaluating contributing factors, and mapping cause-and-effect relationships. By following this structured approach, you will gain the tools and knowledge needed to uncover the root problems and develop targeted solutions. So let's dive into the world of root cause analysis and uncover the hidden factors that lie behind persistent problems.

3.1 IDENTIFYING THE ROOT CAUSE FACTORS

Identifying the root cause factors is a crucial step in the diagnosis process as it helps us understand the underlying reasons behind the persistent problem. By identifying these root cause factors, we can formulate effective solutions that target the source of the problem, rather than just addressing the symptoms.

To identify the root cause factors, we need to employ various tools and techniques that can help us delve deep into the problem. One commonly used tool is the "5 Whys" technique. This technique involves asking "why" multiple times to uncover the underlying cause of the problem. By repeatedly asking "why," we can peel back the layers of symptoms and surface-level issues to reveal the root cause.

For example, let's say that a business is experiencing a high rate of customer churn. The initial problem statement could be: "Customers are cancelling their subscriptions." Using the "5 Whys" technique, we can ask questions such as:

1. Why are customers cancelling their subscriptions? Because they are dissatisfied with the product.
2. Why are they dissatisfied with the product? Because it doesn't meet their expectations.
3. Why doesn't it meet their expectations? Because the product lacks key features.

3.2 EVALUATING CONTRIBUTING FACTORS

In order to effectively address a persistent problem, it is crucial to evaluate the contributing factors that are playing a role in its occurrence. These contributing factors are the underlying causes or conditions that contribute to the problem's existence. By identifying and understanding these factors, you can gain valuable insights into why the problem persists and how it can be resolved.

Evaluating contributing factors requires a systematic approach that involves gathering and analyzing relevant data, as well as utilizing tools and techniques to uncover the root causes. One commonly used tool in evaluating contributing factors is the root cause analysis (RCA), which helps to determine the deeper issues that are responsible for the problem.

During the evaluation process, it is important to consider both internal and external factors that may be contributing to the problem. Internal factors refer to those that are within the control of the individual or organization facing the problem, such as organizational culture, processes, or resources. External factors, on the other hand, are outside of the direct control but still have an impact on the problem, such as market conditions, economic factors, or government regulations.

To illustrate the importance of evaluating contributing factors, let's consider an example of a company experiencing a decline in sales. The company's management may identify a lack of marketing strategies as the root problem. However, by evaluating contributing factors, they may discover that there are external factors such as increased competition or changes in consumer preferences that are also contributing to the decline in sales. By understanding these factors, the company can develop more comprehensive solutions that address both internal and external issues.

In addition to root cause analysis, other techniques that can be used to evaluate contributing factors include fishbone diagrams, Pareto charts, and data analysis methods. These techniques help to identify patterns, trends, and correlations that may shed light on the contributing factors behind a persistent problem.

It is important to note that evaluating contributing factors is an ongoing process and may require continuous monitoring and adjustment. As new information becomes available or circumstances change, the evaluation process should be revisited to ensure that the identified contributing factors are still accurate and relevant.

External references:
- Root Cause Analysis (RCA): https://asq.org/quality-resources/root-cause-analysis

- Fishbone Diagrams - Ishikawa Diagrams: https://www.mindtools.com/pages/articl e/newTMC_05.htm

- Pareto Analysis (Pareto Charts): https://www.projectsmart.co.uk/p areto-analysis-step-by-step.php

3.3 MAPPING CAUSE AND EFFECT RELATIONSHIPS

Mapping cause and effect relationships is a crucial step in the diagnosis process as it helps to identify the underlying factors that contribute to a problem. By understanding these relationships, individuals and businesses can pinpoint the root causes of persistent problems and develop effective solutions.

To map cause and effect relationships, it is essential to analyze the relationships between various factors and their effects on the problem. This involves identifying the factors that directly contribute to the problem, as well as the factors that indirectly influence it.

For example, let's consider a business that is experiencing a decline in customer satisfaction. The direct factors that contribute to this problem could include poor customer service, low product quality, and inefficient processes. These factors directly result in customers being unsatisfied with the business.

However, there may also be indirect factors that influence customer satisfaction. For instance, the lack of employee training and development programs might lead to poor customer service, while outdated equipment and technology could contribute to inefficient processes. By mapping the cause-and-effect relationships between these factors, the business can identify the root causes of the problem and develop appropriate solutions.

One effective method for mapping cause-and-effect relationships is using a cause-and-effect diagram, also known as a fishbone diagram or an Ishikawa diagram. This diagram visually represents the various factors that contribute to a problem, allowing individuals and teams to identify and analyze their relationships.

The cause and effect diagram consists of a horizontal line (the "spine") that represents the problem being studied. Branching off from the spine are several lines, each representing a main cause category. Examples of main cause categories often used in business contexts include people, processes, equipment, materials, environment, and management.

Each main cause category then branches off into smaller lines, representing the specific causes within each category. These specific causes are usually identified through brainstorming sessions and data analysis.

By using a cause-and-effect diagram, individuals and teams can visually map out the various factors contributing to a problem and understand their relationships. This diagram helps to ensure that all potential causes are considered and analyzed, leading to a more comprehensive understanding of the problem and its root causes.

The mapping of cause-and-effect relationships is crucial for effective problem-solving and decision-making. Without understanding these relationships, individuals and businesses may only address the symptoms of a problem instead of tackling the underlying issues. By identifying and analyzing the cause-and-effect relationships, optimal solutions can be developed, leading to sustainable improvements.

External references:
- Using Fishbone Diagrams for Problem Solving: https://asq.org/quality-resources/fishbone
- Cause and Effect Diagram: https://www.mindtools.com/pages/article/newTMC_03.htm

```python
# Example code for creating a cause-and-effect diagram

import matplotlib.pyplot as plt

# Define the main cause categories
main_causes    =    ["People",    "Processes",    "Equipment",
"Materials", "Environment", "Management"]

# Define the specific causes under each category
specific_causes = {
    "People": ["Lack of training", "Inadequate skills", "High
turnover"],
        "Processes": ["Inefficient workflow", "Inconsistent
procedures"],
    "Equipment": ["Outdated technology", "Insufficient tools"],
        "Materials": ["Low-quality materials", "Inaccurate
inventory"],
    "Environment": ["Unsafe working conditions", "Inadequate
lighting"],
    "Management": ["Lack of communication", "Poor decision-
making"]
}

# Plot the cause and effect diagram
plt.figure(figsize=(8, 6))
plt.title("Cause and Effect Diagram: Decline in Customer
Satisfaction")
plt.box(False)
plt.axis("off")
plt.text(0.5, 0.95, "Customer Satisfaction", ha="center",
va="center", fontweight="bold", fontsize=12)
for i, main_cause in enumerate(main_causes):
    y_pos = 0.85 - 0.1 * i
    plt.text(0.075, y_pos, main_cause, ha="left", va="center",
fontweight="bold", fontsize=10)
        for j, specific_cause in
enumerate(specific_causes[main_cause]):
        y_pos = 0.825 - 0.1 * i - 0.025 * j
```

```python
    plt.text(0.075, y_pos, main_cause, ha="left", va="center",
fontweight="bold", fontsize=10)
            for j, specific_cause in
enumerate(specific_causes[main_cause]):
        y_pos = 0.825 - 0.1 * i - 0.025 * j
        plt.text(0.15, y_pos, specific_cause, ha="left", va="center",
fontsize=8)
plt.show()
```

The above example code demonstrates how a cause and effect diagram can be generated using Python's matplotlib library. In this specific example, the diagram represents the causes contributing to a decline in customer satisfaction. The main cause categories are listed on the left side of the diagram, while the specific causes are listed under each category. This visual representation helps to analyze the cause-and-effect relationships and identify potential solutions.

4 GUIDING NEXT STEPS

In this chapter, we will delve into the crucial task of guiding the next steps in solving the identified problem. Once we have clearly defined the problem and articulated the challenges, it is time to prioritize solutions and develop effective action plans. By following this step-by-step process, readers will be equipped with the tools and strategies to move forward confidently towards resolution.

Setting priorities for solutions is an essential part of the next steps. We will explore different methods for evaluating and selecting the most effective approaches to address the root cause of the problem. Additionally, we will discuss how to generate innovative ideas and assess the feasibility of each solution. By understanding these concepts, readers will be able to make informed decisions and choose the optimal path for improvement.

The final part of this chapter will focus on developing action plans. We will discuss the importance of creating detailed and realistic plans that take into account the resources, timeframes, and potential challenges involved. Additionally, we will explore the importance of monitoring and evaluating the progress of the implemented solutions, making adjustments when necessary. By following this chapter's guidance, readers will be empowered to take the necessary steps towards solving their problems and achieving their desired outcomes.

4.1 SETTING PRIORITIES FOR SOLUTIONS

Setting priorities for solutions is an essential step in the problem-solving process. It involves determining which problems need to be addressed first based on their impact and importance. By prioritizing solutions, individuals and businesses can allocate their resources effectively and focus on the most critical issues at hand.

When setting priorities for solutions, it is important to consider several factors:

- Impact: Evaluate the potential impact of each solution on the overall problem. Some solutions may have a greater impact and address the root cause directly, while others may only provide temporary relief. For example, if a business is facing a decline in customer satisfaction, implementing a customer feedback system may have a more significant impact than simply offering discounts.
- Urgency: Consider the urgency of each problem and its solution. Some problems may require immediate attention to prevent further damage or loss. Prioritize these urgent issues to ensure they are resolved promptly. For instance, if a business is experiencing a security breach, addressing it immediately should take precedence over other long-term improvement initiatives.
- Feasibility: Assess the feasibility of implementing each solution. Some solutions may be more realistic and achievable given the available resources, time, and expertise. Prioritize solutions that are feasible and can be implemented effectively. For example, if a business wants to automate its inventory management system, it should evaluate the resources required and the technical capabilities before prioritizing this solution.
- Cost-effectiveness: Consider the cost-effectiveness of each solution. Evaluate the cost of implementation and weigh it against the potential benefits and outcomes. Prioritize solutions that offer the most value for the resources invested. For instance, if a business wants to

to automate its inventory management system, it should evaluate the resources required and the technical capabilities before prioritizing this solution. By considering these factors, individuals and businesses can effectively prioritize solutions and allocate their resources in a way that maximizes the impact and brings about the desired improvements.

Examples:

1. A healthcare organization is facing a high patient attrition rate. After conducting a root cause analysis, they identified long waiting times as a significant factor contributing to the problem. Therefore, they prioritize implementing a more efficient appointment scheduling system to reduce wait times.
2. A manufacturing company is struggling with quality control issues. They identify inadequate training as a root cause. Although there are other ongoing challenges, they prioritize investing in comprehensive training programs for their employees to address this critical factor first.

Setting priorities for solutions requires careful consideration and analysis. It is essential to evaluate each problem's impact, urgency, feasibility, and cost-effectiveness before deciding on the order in which solutions should be implemented.

For additional information on setting priorities for solutions, refer to the following resources:

- Project Management Institute: Setting Priorities: https://www.pmi.org/learning/library/setting-priorities-successful-project-management-6568
- Harvard Business Review: How to Prioritize Your Company's Projects: https://hbr.org/2011/01/how-to-prioritize-your-compan
- Mind Tools: Prioritization Skills for Managers: https://www.mindtools.com/pages/article/newTED_03.htm

4.2 GENERATING INNOVATIVE IDEAS

In order to address the root problems identified through the previous steps, it is crucial to generate innovative ideas that can lead to effective solutions. This section will explore various methods and techniques to spark creativity and generate new and unique ideas.

- **Brainstorming:** Brainstorming is a widely used technique for generating new ideas in a group setting. It involves the free flow of ideas without any judgment or criticism. Participants are encouraged to think outside the box and come up with as many ideas as possible. The goal is to create a diverse range of ideas, which can later be evaluated and refined for implementation. One popular technique within brainstorming is the "5 Whys" method, where the underlying cause of the problem is examined by asking "why" five times. This helps to uncover deeper-rooted issues and generate more innovative solutions.

- **Mind Mapping:** Mind mapping is a visual technique that helps to organize thoughts and ideas. It involves creating a diagram that branches out from a central idea, with each branch representing a different aspect or solution. By visually connecting related ideas and concepts, mind mapping facilitates the generation of innovative ideas. It allows for exploration of various possibilities and connections that may not have been initially apparent. Tools such as MindMeister and XMind can be used to create digital mind maps, which offer collaborative features and easy editing.

- **Reverse Thinking:** Reverse thinking involves approaching a problem from a different perspective. Instead of focusing on finding solutions, this technique encourages thinking about ways to make the problem worse or prevent it from happening. By challenging conventional thinking and exploring the opposite of what is desired, new insights and ideas can emerge. This technique can help break mental barriers and foster innovative and unconventional ideas. For example, if the problem is slow customer service, reverse thinking might involve brainstorming ways to intentionally delay customer responses and analyzing how those scenarios could be mitigated or avoided.

- **Cross-industry Inspiration:** Looking beyond the immediate industry or context of the problem can provide fresh perspectives and inspire innovative solutions. Ideas and practices from other industries or domains can be adapted or modified to address the identified problem. For instance, a manufacturing company facing productivity challenges may find inspiration in lean management practices used in the software development industry. This cross-industry inspiration can lead to the introduction of new concepts and approaches that have not yet been explored within the problem context.

- **Prototype and Test:** Prototyping and testing ideas is an essential part of the innovation process. By creating prototypes of potential solutions, it is possible to validate and refine ideas before full-scale implementation. This approach allows for experimentation and iteration, enabling the identification of potential flaws and improvements. Prototypes can take various forms, ranging from physical models to digital simulations. In the case of software development, rapid prototyping techniques like wireframing or creating interactive mock-ups can be used to gather feedback and refine the solution further.

By incorporating these techniques into the problem-solving process, individuals and businesses can generate innovative ideas that have the potential to address the root problems effectively. It is important to remember that generating ideas is just the starting point, and further evaluation and refinement are necessary before implementing any solution. The next section will explore techniques for assessing the feasibility of the generated ideas and selecting the most suitable ones for implementation.

References:
- Hutchinson, T. (2011). Genius on the cutting edge: The unconventional guide to increasing your intelligence and creativity. Inner Traditions.
- Mind Tools Content Team. (n.d.). Mind Mapping. Retrieved from: https://www.mindtools.com/pages/article/mind-mapping.htm
- Nijssen, E. J., & Frambach, R. T. (2013). Creating customer value through radical innovation. Journal of Marketing, 77(1), 80-96. doi:10.1509/jm.11.0499

4.3 ASSESSING FEASIBILITY OF SOLUTIONS

Once potential solutions have been generated, it is important to assess their feasibility before proceeding with implementation. Assessing feasibility involves evaluating various factors such as cost, time, resources, and potential risks associated with each solution. This step helps in determining which solutions are viable and which ones may not be practical or achievable given the constraints.

One way to assess feasibility is by conducting a cost-benefit analysis. This involves comparing the costs associated with implementing a solution to the potential benefits that it would bring. For example, if the cost of implementing a software upgrade in a business is high, but it would significantly improve efficiency and productivity, then it may be deemed feasible despite the cost.

Another factor to consider in assessing feasibility is the availability of resources. It is important to evaluate whether the necessary resources, such as skilled personnel, equipment, or funding, are readily available or can be obtained within a reasonable timeframe. If a solution requires specialized knowledge or equipment that is not easily accessible, it may not be feasible.

Risk assessment is also an essential part of determining the feasibility of solutions. It is important to identify and evaluate potential risks associated with each solution, considering both the likelihood of the risk occurring and its potential impact. Risk assessment helps in identifying any potential barriers or obstacles that may arise during implementation and allows for the development of mitigation strategies.

External references:

- Cost-Benefit Analysis - Investopedia: https://www.investopedia.com/terms/c/costbenefitanalysis.asp
- Feasibility Study - Project Management Institute: https://www.pmi.org/learning/library/feasibility-study-importance-7304

In summary, assessing feasibility involves evaluating factors such as cost, resources, and risks associated with potential solutions. Conducting a cost-benefit analysis, evaluating resource availability, and identifying potential risks are important steps in assessing the feasibility of solutions. By carefully considering these factors, decision-makers can identify feasible solutions that have the highest likelihood of success.

4.4 DEVELOPING ACTION PLANS

Once the priorities for solutions have been established and innovative ideas have been generated, the next step is to develop action plans. Action plans provide a roadmap for implementing the chosen solutions and ensuring that the identified problems are effectively addressed.

A well-developed action plan outlines the specific steps that need to be taken, assigns responsibilities to individuals or teams, and sets specific deadlines for completion. It is a detailed guide that helps in organizing and executing the necessary actions for problem resolution.

To develop action plans, it is important to consider the following:

- **Clearly define the objectives:** Clearly articulate the desired outcomes that the action plans aim to achieve. This ensures that the actions taken align with the overall goals and objectives of addressing the root problem.
- **Break down the actions into smaller tasks:** Break down the main actions into smaller, manageable tasks. This helps in assigning responsibilities and tracking progress more effectively.
- **Assign responsibilities:** Clearly assign responsibilities to individuals or teams for each task. This ensures accountability and helps in ensuring that the action plan is executed efficiently.
- **Set deadlines:** Set specific deadlines for each task to ensure timely completion. Deadlines create a sense of urgency and help maintain momentum throughout the implementation process.
- **Consider resource requirements:** Identify the resources, such as personnel, budget, or equipment, needed for each task. This helps in ensuring that the necessary resources are allocated and available when needed.

- **Monitor and measure progress:** Regularly monitor and measure progress against the action plan. This helps in identifying any deviations or issues early on and allows for timely adjustments.
- **Communicate and collaborate:** Foster open communication and collaboration among all stakeholders involved in the action plan. Regular updates and feedback sessions help in keeping everyone aligned and motivated towards achieving the desired outcomes.

It is also important to note that action plans may need to be flexible to accommodate unforeseen challenges or changes in circumstances. Regular evaluation and adjustment of the action plans will help in keeping them relevant and effective.

For example, let's say a small business is facing the challenge of declining customer satisfaction due to slow response times to customer inquiries. After analyzing the root causes, the business decides to implement the solution of improving customer service by hiring additional customer support staff. The action plan for this solution may include tasks such as:

- **Task 1:** Conduct a market analysis to determine the optimal number of customer support representatives required.
- **Task 2:** Recruit and hire additional support staff within the next two months.
- **Task 3:** Provide training to the new staff on company procedures and customer service best practices.
- **Task 4:** Implement a new ticketing system to streamline customer inquiries and ensure timely response.
- **Task 5:** Monitor customer response times and satisfaction levels on a weekly basis.
- **Task 6:** Evaluate the effectiveness of the new customer service initiatives after three months and make adjustments as needed.

By following these action plan tasks and monitoring progress, the business can effectively address the root problem of slow customer response times and improve customer satisfaction.

References:

- "Developing an Action Plan" by Community Tool Box, University of Kansas: https://ctb.ku.edu/en/table-of-contents/overview/plan-do-study-act/develop-action-plans/main
- "Creating an Action Plan for Business Growth" by Business Queensland, Queensland Government: https://www.business.qld.gov.au/starting-business/planning/market-customer-research/action-plans

5 IMPLEMENTING OPTIMAL SOLUTIONS

Implementing Optimal Solutions is a crucial step in the process of addressing persistent problems. After identifying the root causes and developing action plans, this chapter focuses on the execution of those plans and the subsequent monitoring and evaluation. It provides readers with guidance on how to effectively implement their chosen solutions and make necessary adjustments along the way.

In this chapter, we will explore the importance of executing action plans and the role of monitoring and evaluation in ensuring the success of implemented solutions. We will also discuss how to stay proactive and adaptive during the implementation process, making adjustments as needed to ensure optimal outcomes. By the end of this chapter, readers will have a clear understanding of the steps involved in implementing optimal solutions and will be equipped with the knowledge and tools to effectively execute their own action plans.

5.1 EXECUTION OF ACTION PLANS

Once the optimal solutions have been identified, the next step is to execute the action plans that will address the root causes of the persistent problem. This involves implementing the proposed solutions and monitoring their progress. Execution of action plans requires careful planning and coordination. It is important to assign responsibility to specific individuals or teams who will be responsible for carrying out the action plans. Clear communication and regular updates are crucial to ensure everyone understands their roles and responsibilities.

To illustrate the execution of action plans, let's consider an example of a small business that is experiencing declining sales. After identifying the root causes and generating innovative ideas, the business owners decide to implement the following action plans:

1. **Improving the website:** The business realises that their website is outdated and not optimised for mobile devices. To address this, they hire a web developer to revamp the website and make it more user-friendly and responsive. They set a specific timeline for the completion of the website redesign.

2. **Enhancing customer service:** The business recognizes that poor customer service may be impacting their sales. They decide to provide training to their employees on effective communication and problem-solving skills. They also implement a customer feedback system to track customer satisfaction and address any issues promptly.

3. **Increasing marketing efforts:** The business understands the importance of promoting their products and services to attract new customers. They develop a comprehensive marketing plan that includes social media advertising, email marketing campaigns, and collaborations with local influencers. They allocate a budget for their marketing activities and monitor the performance of each campaign.

5.1 EXECUTION OF ACTION PLANS

Once the optimal solutions have been identified, the next step is to execute the action plans that will address the root causes of the persistent problem. This involves implementing the proposed solutions and monitoring their progress. Execution of action plans requires careful planning and coordination. It is important to assign responsibility to specific individuals or teams who will be responsible for carrying out the action plans. Clear communication and regular updates are crucial to ensure everyone understands their roles and responsibilities.

To illustrate the execution of action plans, let's consider an example of a small business that is experiencing declining sales. After identifying the root causes and generating innovative ideas, the business owners decide to implement the following action plans:

1. **Improving the website:** The business realises that their website is outdated and not optimised for mobile devices. To address this, they hire a web developer to revamp the website and make it more user-friendly and responsive. They set a specific timeline for the completion of the website redesign.

2. **Enhancing customer service:** The business recognizes that poor customer service may be impacting their sales. They decided to provide training to their employees on effective communication and problem-solving skills. They also implement a customer feedback system to track customer satisfaction and address any issues promptly.

3. **Increasing marketing efforts:** The business understands the importance of promoting their products and services to attract new customers. They develop a comprehensive marketing plan that includes social media advertising, email marketing campaigns, and collaborations with local influencers. They allocate a budget for their marketing activities and monitor the performance of each campaign.

Throughout the execution of these action plans, the business regularly tracks their progress and evaluates the effectiveness of each solution. They gather data on website traffic, customer feedback, and sales metrics to measure the impact of the implemented changes. If necessary, adjustments are made to the action plans based on the results obtained.

It is important to note that the execution of action plans is not a one-time event. It requires ongoing monitoring and evaluation to ensure that the implemented solutions are producing the expected results. Regular communication and feedback loops are essential to address any challenges or roadblocks that may arise during the execution phase.

External References:
- For more information on the execution of action plans in business, you can refer to this article: Execution: The Discipline of Getting Things Done: https://hbr.org/2002/06/execution-the-discipline-of-getting-things-done
- To learn about effective project management techniques, the Project Management Institute provides valuable resources: Project Management Institute: https://www.pmi.org/
- This article offers insights on monitoring and evaluating action plans to achieve organizational goals: Monitoring and Evaluation: Some Tools, Methods and Approaches: https://www.nber.org/papers/w15429.pdf

5.2 MONITORING AND EVALUATION

After the implementation of the action plans, it is crucial to monitor and evaluate their effectiveness in resolving the identified problems. Monitoring and evaluation enable us to assess the progress made, identify any gaps or shortcomings, and make necessary adjustments to optimize the solutions. This section will discuss the importance of monitoring and evaluation, provide examples of monitoring and evaluation techniques, and offer guidance on how to effectively conduct these processes.

Importance of Monitoring and Evaluation

Monitoring and evaluation play a vital role in ensuring the success of the implemented solutions. They allow us to measure the impact of the actions taken and determine whether the desired outcomes are being achieved. Without proper monitoring and evaluation, it becomes difficult to identify if the solutions are working as intended or if any further modifications are required.

Monitoring involves the systematic collection of data and information on the progress of the solutions. It helps us track the implementation process, identify any unexpected issues or barriers, and keep stakeholders informed about the status of the problem-solving efforts. On the other hand, evaluation involves the systematic assessment of the effectiveness and efficiency of the implemented solutions. It helps us understand the overall impact of the actions taken, whether they have addressed the root causes, and if they have improved the situation for the better.

Examples of Monitoring and Evaluation Techniques

1. **Quantitative and Qualitative Data Collection:** Monitoring and evaluation can involve gathering both quantitative and qualitative data. Quantitative data includes numbers, statistics, and measurable indicators, while qualitative data focuses on subjective experiences and perceptions. For example, in a business context, quantitative data may include sales figures, customer satisfaction ratings, and productivity metrics. Qualitative data, on the other hand, may involve surveys, interviews, and feedback from employees or customers.

2. **Key Performance Indicators (KPIs):** KPIs are specific metrics or indicators that measure the progress and success of the implemented solutions. They provide a quantitative way to assess whether the desired outcomes are being achieved. For instance, in a personal context, a KPI for weight loss could be the number of pounds lost or the reduction in body fat percentage. In a business context, a KPI could be an increase in profit margins or a decrease in customer complaints.

3. **Surveys and Feedback Mechanisms:** Surveys and feedback mechanisms are valuable tools for collecting qualitative data and gathering insights from stakeholders. They allow individuals to express their opinions, suggestions, and concerns about the implemented solutions. Surveys can be conducted through online platforms or in-person interviews, while feedback mechanisms can leverage technologies such as suggestion boxes or dedicated communication channels.

4. **Benchmarking:** Benchmarking involves comparing the performance of the implemented solutions against industry standards or best practices. It helps assess whether the solutions are meeting or exceeding expectations. Benchmarking can highlight areas of improvement and provide insights into innovations or strategies adopted by other individuals or organizations facing similar problems.

Guidelines for Effective Monitoring and Evaluation

To ensure the effectiveness of monitoring and evaluation processes, here are some guidelines to follow:

1. **Define Clear Evaluation Criteria:** Clearly define the criteria and standards against which the solutions will be evaluated. This includes setting specific goals and objectives, determining relevant indicators, and establishing a baseline to measure progress.
2. **Establish a Monitoring Schedule:** Develop a schedule for regular monitoring activities to track the progress of the implemented solutions. This could involve weekly, monthly, or quarterly check-ins depending on the nature of the problem and the expected timeline for improvement.
3. **Engage Stakeholders:** Involve stakeholders throughout the monitoring and evaluation processes. Seek their input, listen to their feedback, and consider their perspectives when assessing the effectiveness of the solutions. This engagement can enhance buy-in and support for problem-solving efforts.
4. **Use Multiple Evaluation Methods:** Use a combination of quantitative and qualitative evaluation methods to obtain a comprehensive view of the results. This ensures a more holistic assessment of the solutions and provides deeper insights into their impact.
5. **Adapt and Adjust as Needed:** Continuously monitor the progress and outcomes of the implemented solutions and be prepared to make adjustments if necessary. Flexibility is key in problem-solving, as it allows for the incorporation of new information and the modification of strategies to ensure optimal results.

References

- World Bank Group. (2004). Monitoring and evaluation: Some tools, methods and approaches: https://openknowledge.worldbank.org/handle/10986/15085
- United Nations Development Programme. (2016). Handbook on Planning, Monitoring and Evaluating for Development Results: https://www.undp.org/content/dam/aplaws/publication/en/publications/poverty-reduction/handbook-on-planning-monitoring-and-evaluating-for-development-results/UNDP-PME-handbook-2016.pdf

5.3 MAKING ADJUSTMENTS AS NEEDED

Once the optimal solutions have been implemented, it is important to continuously monitor and evaluate their effectiveness. This process involves making adjustments as needed to ensure that the desired improvements are being achieved.

Making adjustments can involve a variety of actions, including modifying the implemented solutions, refining action plans, and reassessing feasibility. By regularly reviewing the progress and impact of the solutions, it becomes possible to identify any areas that require further attention or modification.

For example, suppose a business identified a problem of low customer satisfaction and implemented a new customer service training program. After a few months, the business notices that customer satisfaction scores have improved but not as significantly as desired. In this case, the business would need to make adjustments to the training program by incorporating additional customer feedback or consulting external resources for best practices in customer service.

Another example could be a personal problem of chronic back pain. A person may start implementing stretching exercises recommended by a physical therapist. However, they may find that the exercises are not providing the expected relief. In this situation, the person should make adjustments by consulting with the physical therapist to modify the exercises or explore alternative treatment options. Making adjustments as needed is essential for ensuring that the solutions remain effective and efficient. It allows for ongoing improvement and adaptation, ensuring that the root problem is fully addressed and resolved.

External references:

- "Change Management Principles: Don't Forget the Adjustment Phase" by Project Management Institute: https://www.pmi.org/learning/library/dont-forget-adjustment-phase-change-management-4491
- "The Importance of Continuous Improvement in Problem Solving" by Lean Enterprise Institute: https://www.lean.org/WhatareYouDoing/ViewAllBlogs.cfm?PublishedRange=0&Digest=no&AuthorLastName=Peterson&BlogStartDate=01/01/2020&BlogEndDate=12/31/2020&AuthorID=9503800&SearchListMethod=AND&partialsearch=i

CONCLUSION

CONCLUSION

As we reach the final pages of "The Diagnosis," I hope you've found the journey through this self-help book to be illuminating and empowering. Throughout these chapters, we've embarked on a quest to better understand the intricate web of factors that influence our personal lives and businesses. We've delved into the art of diagnosis, seeking to uncover the root causes that often lie beneath the surface, waiting to be revealed.

In the world of medicine, a proper diagnosis is the crucial first step toward effective treatment and healing. Similarly, in our personal lives and businesses, identifying the root causes of our challenges and successes is the key to making meaningful improvements and achieving lasting growth. "The Diagnosis" was designed to be your guide on this transformative journey of self-discovery and improvement.

The Power of Self-Reflection

Throughout this book, we've explored various tools, techniques, and strategies for diagnosis, all of which are grounded in the fundamental power of self-reflection. Self-awareness is the cornerstone of personal and professional growth. By taking the time to examine our thoughts, behaviours, and circumstances, we unlock the potential for profound transformation.

Uncovering Root Causes

We've delved into the depths of our personal and business challenges, uncovering root causes that may have long been hidden from view. We've learned that these root causes can take many forms – from deeply ingrained beliefs and habits to external factors beyond our control. By shining a light on these hidden drivers, we gain the power to address them and effect positive change.

Implementing Change

Diagnosis is not an end in itself but a means to an end. Armed with a deeper understanding of the factors influencing our lives and businesses, we're now equipped to take action. We've explored strategies for setting and achieving meaningful goals, building resilience, and fostering positive relationships – all essential components of personal and professional success.

The Ongoing Journey

It's important to remember that the journey of diagnosis and self-improvement is ongoing. Life and business are dynamic, and continually evolving, and so too must our understanding and strategies evolve with them. Embrace the process of self-discovery as a lifelong adventure, and approach it with an open heart and a curious mind.

As you close the final chapter of "The Diagnosis," I encourage you to take the insights and tools you've gained and apply them with intentionality and determination. Use the power of diagnosis to navigate the challenges that lie ahead and to celebrate the successes that await you. Remember that you have the ability to shape your personal life and business in ways that align with your true desires and values.

Thank you for embarking on this journey with me. May your path be filled with self-awareness, growth, and the fulfilment of your deepest aspirations. May you continue to diagnose, understand, and transform your world, one revelation at a time.

With warmest regards,

Sabrina Ben Salmi

Author, "The Diagnosis"

Always remember...

We Are All Connected!

**Trust your highest thought,
your clearest words and your
grandest feeling. Your highest
thought is always the thought
which makes you feel good.
Your clearest words are the
words which contain truth and
honesty. Your grandest feeling
is LOVE**

**Have a wonderful day enjoying
your unique dance with life.**

JOURNAL

GIVE YOURSELF TIME JOURNAL

Within this section of this book, you will delve into the power of journaling for success.

In the fast-paced world we live in today, achieving success can often feel like an uphill battle. We're bombarded with information, distractions, and competing demands on our time. It's no wonder that many of us struggle to attain our desired outcomes, whether in our careers, personal lives, or health and well-being. But fear not, for within this section of this book, you will discover a powerful tool that can help you navigate this journey to success: the art of journaling.

Journaling is not just a mere act of putting pen to paper; it's a proven method for self-improvement, personal growth, and achieving your goals. Over the years, countless individuals, from scientists and artists to entrepreneurs and athletes, have harnessed the transformative power of journaling to unlock their full potential and attain the success you desire. In this chapter, we will explore the science behind journaling and how it can become an indispensable habit on your path to success.

The Science of Journaling

Before we dive into the practical aspects of journaling, it's essential to understand why it works. The act of journaling taps into the profound connection between the mind and the written word. It's a process that goes beyond simply recording your thoughts; it engages your brain in a way that enhances self-awareness, problem-solving, and goal achievement.

Research in psychology and neuroscience has shown that journaling can have several profound effects on the human mind:

1. **Clarification of Thoughts:** When you write down your thoughts and feelings, you clarify them. You give form to the abstract, making it easier to process and understand.
2. **Stress Reduction:** Journaling can be a form of emotional release. It allows you to vent your frustrations and fears, reducing stress and promoting emotional well-being.
3. **Goal Setting and Achievement:** Writing down your goals makes them tangible and concrete. This act alone increases your commitment to achieving them.
4. **Self-Reflection:** Regular journaling encourages self-reflection. You can track your progress, identify patterns in your behaviour, and make informed decisions for personal growth.
5. **Problem Solving:** Journaling can help you tackle complex problems by allowing you to break them down into smaller, manageable parts.
6. **Increased Focus and Productivity:** The act of journaling can help you clarify your priorities and stay focused on what truly matters, ultimately boosting your productivity.

The Journaling Habit: Your Key to Success

Now that you understand the science behind journaling, it's time to embrace it as a habit on your journey to success. Think of your journal as a trusted companion on this path, always there to help you navigate challenges, set clear goals, and stay accountable to yourself.

To get started, consider the following tips:

- **Set Clear Intentions:** Begin your journaling journey with a clear purpose in mind. What do you want to achieve? What are your long-term and short-term goals? Knowing your intentions will give your journaling practice direction.
- **Consistency is Key:** Establish a regular journaling routine. Whether it's daily, weekly, or monthly, consistency will help you reap the maximum benefits of this practice.
- **Write Freely:** Don't hold back. Write whatever comes to mind without judgment. Your journal is a safe space for your thoughts and feelings.
- **Track Progress:** Use your journal to track your progress toward your goals. Celebrate your achievements, no matter how small they may seem.
- **Reflect and Learn:** Take time to reflect on your journal entries. What insights can you glean from them? What can you learn from your past experiences?

As you embark on your journaling journey, remember that this is a scientifically proven method to increase your chances of success. By making journaling a regular habit, you are equipping yourself with a powerful tool that can help you overcome obstacles, stay focused on your goals, and ultimately achieve the success you desire.

Success is within your reach, and journaling is your map to get there.

THE DIAGNOSIS

THE DIAGNOSIS

THE DIAGNOSIS

THE DIAGNOSIS

THE DIAGNOSIS

THE DIAGNOSIS

GIVE YOURSELF TIME JOUURNAL

THE DIAGNOSIS

THE DIAGNOSIS

THE DIAGNOSIS

THE DIAGNOSIS

THE DIAGNOSIS

THE DIAGNOSIS

GIVE YOURSELF TIME JOURNAL

THE DIAGNOSIS

THE DIAGNOSIS

THE DIAGNOSIS

THE DIAGNOSIS

THE DIAGNOSIS

THE DIAGNOSIS

ABOUT THE AUTHOR

Sabrina Ben Salmi (AKA Mum) is a multi-award winning author, publisher, public speaker

Sabrinas' purpose is to transform the narrative of parenting for over 1 million families.

Sabrina is a UN Women UK Delegate for the CSW76 alongside her eldest daughter Lashai Ben Salmi and eldest son Tray-Sean Ben Salmi.

Sabrina is the winner of the Black Achievement Award - Best Dyslexic Owned Business 2021.

Sabrina is a proud mother of 5 multiple award-winning authors, publishers, public speakers, consultants and presenters.

Sabrina has also been recognised as No 2 on the list of Top 50 Most Inspirational Black Women in the UK 2019 (https://www.voice-online.co.uk/news/uk-news/2019/11/16/university-lecturer-makes-list-of-top-50-inspirational-black-women/). Sabrina helps families to DREAM BIG TOGETHER and write their stories as they build their family legacy.

Sabrina Ben Salmi is a Podcast Host on Life According To Sabrina: https://sabrinabensalmi.sounder.fm/show/life-according-to-sabrina-ben-salmi

Sabrina is an RSA FELLOW (Royal Society of Arts).

ABOUT *The* AUTHOR

MEET THE MIND
BEHIND THE METHOD
HTTPS://LINKTR.EE/SABRINABENSALMI

Sabrina Ben Salmi (AKA Mum) was invited to write an article on 'The importance of diversity and inclusion in boardrooms' that was featured in Arabian Business:
https://www.arabianbusiness.com/spotlight/the-importance-of-diversity-and-inclusion-in-boardrooms

Sabrina was invited to write an article on 'Youth of today leaders of tomorrow' that was featured in Arabian Business:
https://www.arabianbusiness.com/spotlight/youth-of-today-leaders-of-tomorrow

Sabrina has been a Support Panel Member for UnLtd

Sabrina was 1 out of 6 to be shortlisted for The Marcus Garvey Award 2020 on December 19th at West Side Young Leaders Academy's Annual Wakwanzaa celebration

The Ben Salmi family were acknowledged during the Chelsea FC - Edge of The Box 6th Anniversary celebration:
https://www.chelseafc.com/en/news/2021/12/15/edge-of-the-box-club-celebrates-six-year-anniversary

Brunel University London (B.U.L) has given the Ben Salmi family the opportunity to participate in Masterclasses covering Engineering, Computer Science and currently the Environmental Agency Masterclass.

Let's STAY CONNECTED

HTTPS://LINKTR.EE/SABRINABENSALMI

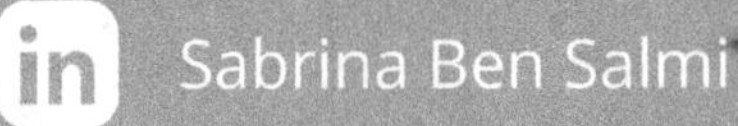

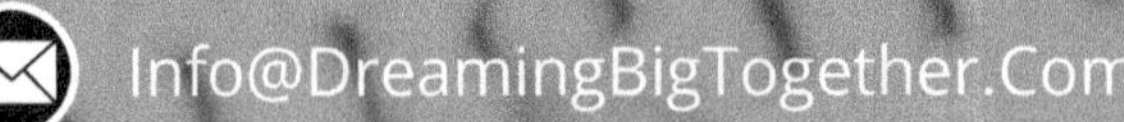

" GET TO THE ROOT CAUSE

www.ingramcontent.com/pod-product-compliance
Lightning Source LLC
Chambersburg PA
CBHW080458030726
47592CB00011B/3173